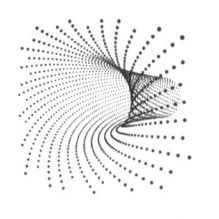

**FIRSTMATTERPRESS**
Portland, Ore.

**ALSO BY K. M. LIGHTHOUSE**

*Time Counts Backward From Infinity*
*You Are An Ambiguous Pronoun*
*The Observer Effect*

# BODY
# UNTIL
# LIGHT

Copyright © 2020 by K. M. Lighthouse
All rights reserved

Published in the United States
by First Matter Press
Portland, Oregon

Paperback ISBN 978-1-7338246-1-3

Edited by Lauren Paredes,
Caroline Wilcox Reul & Ash Good

Cover Illustration
Copyright © 2020 by Sara Swoboda
@continuous_drawing_project

Book design & typography
by Ash Good www.ashgood.design

FIRSTMATTERPRESS.ORG

# BODY UNTIL LIGHT

k. m. lighthouse

**FIRSTMATTERPRESS**
Portland, Ore.

## CONTENTS

- 9    Hand-Me-Down Addictions
- 10    Improve the World
- 11    This Magic Is Ready for You
- 13    Shadow Dancer
- 15    One-man Band on Tour
- 17    Your Ancestors Are
- 18    Careless Clockwork Deities and Gods of Living Art
- 20    Remember Your Dreams
- 21    Integrate
- 23    Interlude: One Breath as Silence Echoes
- 24    Birth This Body
- 26    Sleeping on the Wrong Pillow
- 28    Particle Collision
- 30    What Sensei Says to You
- 32    Fold the Universe
- 34    Body of Language

| | |
|---|---|
| 37 | Both Poison and Cure |
| 39 | You Decide Today Is a Good Day |
| 41 | The Ground Listens to You |
| 43 | What Happens When You Stop Mistaking Shared Loneliness for Love |
| 45 | Lay with Universes on the Backs of Your Eyes |
| 47 | Time to Turn Chameleon |
| 48 | Self-Sovereign |
| 49 | What Appears to Be Death |
| 51 | Don't Leave Until the Candle Goes Out |
| 53 | Midnight Creators' Conference |
| 54 | Be the World You Want to See Change |
| | |
| 57 | Acknowledgments |

# HAND-ME-DOWN ADDICTIONS

Welcome
Welcome to the soft drowsiness of denial
      the stubborn lethargy of falling deeper

into your body      Welcome
to disappearance      the forgetting
of what makes you human

Recognize your impatient fog
      the shaky dialogue of cold fingers      Welcome
to your own underbelly

where disembodied mermaids pretend
not to sing of your sorrows
      or else soften them with the beauty of sound

The salt on your fingertips never felt so good
—this is your inheritance      cosmic alignment
of stars so you can forget fate

You come alone to where even ice
tastes like tequila and all you have to contemplate
is flat beer and the emptiness of atoms

## IMPROVE THE WORLD

You create an alternate universe
where buses arrive
on time          where
Grandpa responds to your letters
and you are friends
with all your one-time lovers     You create
an alternate universe where your cat stops
aggravating squirrels
and flea beetles
stay away from your porch garden
You create an alternate universe
where the homeless
people talking in that tent
don't need the walker outside it
and the rest of Portland's streets
are alphabetical
You create
an alternate
universe
where

# THIS MAGIC IS READY FOR YOU

You stand in the center
of fifty hypnotized
people who await
your suggestion          You
could so easily

orchestrate
their oh-so-visible
desires          hand-pick
some inner circle
You wonder how

so many of them
are eager for
some temporary
direction toward
salvation          satisfaction

        solemnity
And do you imagine
yourself
an impartial judge          oh
God of Fate?

No     but you still
choose
who will go
when the paths
forward glow

like landing strips
on a clear night
      —everyone
already standing
in an improvised

pentagram
position

## SHADOW DANCER

You enter a circle of white
candles that drip from unequal lengths

as they cast
contorted      engorged shadows

Your limbs move to examine every angle
of themselves simultaneously

      all but featureless in the melding
reflection of candlelight's gray scale

Your naked hips and arms fall in
and out of synchrony

with flame as it substantiates
the breath of the room itself

      enough to understand
intimacy      bathed in the displaced light

of existence    —a flicker
in the realm of creation

The walls expand and contract to meet
locations of your body that       if drawn

          would require the shading
of deep charcoal

Eyelashes become unrecognizable
          and your shadowed head separates

across two dimensions    —thin slices of shape—
exchanging themselves for an infinity

of hands and fingers
Your eyes are closed

in the hardly perceptible loss
of unity and oxygen

This is the performance of dying
in small amounts:

you paint with the absence
of light

# ONE-MAN BAND ON TOUR

You watch him play guitar
                with a credit card

In his sound      the whole

of existence fell away        swallowed
by the gaping maw

      of raw space between notes    —milliseconds—
when you hear other dimensions
    call
        and bleed through

You follow him to a restaurant where
he uses the credit card
    and leaves
it there
    tosses his keys    —glints of metal against stars—
    to a startled homeless man
        and starts walking

His Rocketdog feet are the first to go
      and legs next    discorporate
        now part of pavement

He was only passing through             —a musical delusion—
leaving
          the guitar cacophony of strings on ground
                    reverberating downtown

## YOUR ANCESTORS ARE

Spider mother
has forgotten herself and laughs

as strings descend from her center
to unfold and give birth to marionettes

        these skeletons of dress        Not one strand
            but many     and still she laughs and crests

these lavender skies without direction    They say
she gives birth to monsters

in her eternity and exists
as a noise-song underneath consensus

reality        but you have been her womb
      surrogate for idea rebirth     a pendulum

of momentum that borrowed rhythm from your footsteps
and harbored space to unwind the clockmaker god

## CARELESS CLOCKWORK DEITIES AND GODS OF LIVING ART

You should have known not to sleep
               on the blanket of your birth
     In this shared dream
you throw seeds on fertile ground
               and forget to watch them grow        left
to the weeds and withering of time—

Do you remember
       the pretty things you said
              among stars about places you had
travelled? Where you once swallowed
       love spiders in your sleep                or
wished to be readmitted
       into those circular caves dripping
fluids of distant thought?
       There           with barely fireflies to see by
you walked a path you knew
along the corridors
of your body         weaving
       under and over tendons and flesh
             memories and rolling hills

Past the garden        the children rotate
        on the Möbius strip playground
                and disappear
into another dimension
        when their mind-purse mothers come to call
      You like to think one of those children was yours
        the somber    recycled one who knows
        his purpose was an accident
—he will probably need glasses soon

You see him again and realize
        what makes a person beautiful is the attempt—
missing is the point

# REMEMBER YOUR DREAMS

Between possibilities of eagle and the silence of the moon
        you have six arms and three legs outstretched
        on a ball that rolls down the balance beam of analysis
        in these dreams that make dreams out of life

Here you think your entire life is a day         a day
the way god created the world in seven
And     if your life is a single day
        then this       too     will pass into the ocean of stars
where no energy is lost and *nothing* is gained

But the thing about days is that they repeat
        repeat themselves in the déjà vu of worlds
ending and beginning again between breaths
even when you forget to breathe from the stomach

        and fall top-heavy into a bedroom messy
            with days gone by     until it's morning again
The cats wake you up with each of their nine lives
        and the gentle pouring of dry food sounds like a rainmaker
                      from the bathroom

# INTEGRATE


Having left heartbeats

ghosts          time-stamped versions
of who you were just that moment ago

call them again into being
simultaneously        summon
those selves up from the ground        Beckon

them within until your timelines tip up
on themselves and there is no forward
or backward     —only upward—
only what stacks upon itself

into great towers of existence
                Here         everything is tangled
and connected       crossing and retreading
paths wound around each other
and never touching

Or when touch happens
        as you balance the great structure
                of future history
                        within your goose-bumped flesh
it is only to trade floors
of memories
for others      fostered now
in foreign bodies as they rotate
back toward the ground     land
on this plane      and whisper
to time      *stop*
*standing so still*

## INTERLUDE: ONE BREATH AS SILENCE ECHOES

in this monumental soundscape      rounded
waves of frequency your mind translates
into reality      fluctuations of vibration
in notes that sing      *—express*
There are colors here    too
      the soft gray of interaction with a body
        the elegant purple of language
about to be born

# BIRTH THIS BODY

Where the beak goes
       the body follows
in its passage through cracks in skin-glass
       these observation tanks of embryonic fluid

and awareness       amnesiac egg shells    Push through
       and out
holes the size of puckered mouths
       escape

one enclosed world for another where you have forgotten
how to breathe or     perhaps     were forbidden
       to speak
       Tense and contract    push    squeeze

hold       release into the never-ending folds
of your compact shape     your features of evolution
in conversation with the surface of your skin
Now       pretend to know how to move

in this body: first left hip rotates by degrees
to stretch     blink      hold position
       then shift to right
when socially acceptable     Repeat

Keep arms steady
to create the illusion you can stay still
You grow and wait to remember before
        when love makes you
and not the other way around

until your own pleasures
are again the birth
of you

## SLEEPING ON THE WRONG PILLOW


A headache           —debilitating
         this cosmic shift
of a migraine that borders
         a pain high
    from reality

The center of your bedroom
tapestry
—hanging from the ceiling
    with thumbtacks—
        fades in and out
of lavender purple
and gold

The edges
    melt
          darkness in peripherals
      every sensation too much     —light lilac
perfume from the girl with her window
      down       sun through clouds     crickets
chirping

Indistinguishable mass of life
               and movement        galaxy colors
                   bursting eyes
     —stars in daylight—
             this biological hallucinogen

# PARTICLE COLLISION

Your bedroom body doesn't want clothes

doesn't want touch either     maybe later
    maybe when the gnawing desire for almost

fades into the hours that pass

while you are not touching but generate
movement inside body     You translate

almost-touch into electricity textures and remember

that nothing ever truly touches    —it's just empty space
at the level of molecules—    so you heighten

this contact mirage until you want

what does not exist and decide to pretend it does
Embrace in the center of tiny lights emitted

in cell communication and pull attention to skin surface

where suddenly there are fingertips and colors
made of stars     suddenly there are visions

behind open eyes as you stare at the ceiling       suddenly

there is nothing wrong behind doors
where you don't touch until touch is all you are

       borders blurring at poorly defined edges

# WHAT SENSEI SAYS TO YOU


You understand he needs no eyes to see learning
       —his hands guide you to the ground
where you roll and return to your feet     His focus    floats
as he roots around your arms and flicks
his wrist with a relaxed
                sigh that collapses legs

He says
            you won't believe him
            until it happens
to you

When you take the defensive stance
and he punches     you locate
the mechanism to unhinge
balance     He falls     grinning

*Fold up just like origami*     he says
as you roll forward     You practice more
times than you say you will and forget
to exhale     ribs sore from storage

Later everything is a lock
that opens when pushed
with blind fingers
so you root around
possibility slide out of and into
place

Your arms are alive with travel in swelling waves
while the group blooms
and returns to seed Blooms
and returns to seed

Blooms and
blooms
and blooms

# FOLD THE UNIVERSE

You stare at water
as it slaps against a lover's hand          reading palm lines
to copy the message
       wavelengths held together with hydrogen bonds

Their voice
       —air-amplified rhythms
            that reach for your ears and surge
                 through folds in your brain—
travels while neurons      synapses
       tirelessly unwind memories
            and make creases for new ones

Their wallpaper is coming off in the corners
       folded like pages of a well-loved book
            dog-eared here and
     here                  and here

When your body folds into theirs          you want them
to remember            *—encircle me as I encircle you—*
      *press me into your muscles so I leave an imprint*
      *in your winding DNA*
           *if only until cells you have now are exchanged*
for others

*Leave the wrinkles in your shirt today*
*—they hold onto you like I do*

# BODY OF LANGUAGE

When you are a being a metaphor
        some core portion of your identity

unable to separate symbol
from reality     literal from iconic

        you find yourself easily transported
            so when someone you don't know

says       *could you imagine being*
*with those people?* You *can*

        suddenly intruding on some strangers'
family dinner as a presence or poltergeist

with no extra place setting
to know if you're welcome     Or

when you remember how trees
share nutrients underground

while staring at a telephone pole
inches from forest     see its body

full of staples and rusted nails
and wonder if the trees mistake

this deadened wood for one of their own
You grow angry at this mistreatment

until you *are* the pole      alive
by just a sliver inside    crucified flesh

with decomposing shreds of
some other tree's paper

hanging from one side
And when you are a body of water

attempting to explain the ineffable
—how you perceive color or

what *is* the sensation of orgasm?—
you find only images: two myceliary streams

of water forming some unnamed river
to describe the oxymoronic convergence of

platonic and sexual       god and
self      intention and accident

And somehow it is this inelegance of language
that makes you fall in love with life again

      headfirst into the merger of
conceptual opposites

and their awkward physical forms

# BOTH POISON AND CURE

A being with no story approaches
and asks you to make them believe
in anything

You tell them it's easiest
when they *want* to believe
and so begin

by cupping their head
in both your hands
and avoiding eye contact          Add

pressure here and then
there          discovering
all the places their body has forgotten

the pain it tenses around          Press down
a little harder before releasing
this mechanical reset

button          *Have you tried
turning it off and back on again?*
But sometimes it takes a person

opposite you to remind you
to believe your own healing
        someone to squeeze between thumb

and forefinger         vibrate over
right-side collarbone         and assure you
this time machine knows when to repair itself

## YOU DECIDE TODAY IS A GOOD DAY

and even light
through the crack in a door
winks at you    playful
and beckoning

*What compels*
*you?* it asks
as even the ground sparkles
So turn the music up today    flip

all the lights on    laugh at the way
confused cats stare up
at your mirth    There is little reason
for this ecstasy except

that you wrote that word
in condensation on your glass
shower door and feel
everything

in some wild afterglow
You feel your menstrual blood
  escaping    a bowling ball
of pressure sliding down

        but even those muscle contractions
return you to awe and excitement
        your body a roller coaster of sensation
you *must* listen to        You are giddy

all night on the coattails of being content
with this mystery
        and ask a lover to hold a hand
over your uterus because

the movement is so strong that        surely
        it is possible to sense it from the outside
And somehow        there is grace
in this moment        a sense of creation

        renewal in what wasn't a child
        and as you press your cramping belly
        into the small of your lover's back
        you can't help but feel them

carrying this miraculous event
with you as you fade        rocked
to sleep by the involuntary motions
of your body

# THE GROUND LISTENS TO YOU

*Buzz buzz buzz* in your fingers
with nowhere for this vibration

to go except where you play notes
across another body     composing

some childish melody
into the peach fuzz of someone's back

This stranger is soft and responsive
as you nuzzle this energy

into the crook of their neck     fast
now to keep pace

with some playful speed
of pleasure

You begin to feel into your fur
      hair sprouting and spiny

as it rubs across a leg     foot
      eliciting giggles so you know

this buzzing is contagious
        these electric ripples metered

to a distant      thunderous
drumbeat            the sound of

the metronome Earth
keeping time

## WHAT HAPPENS WHEN YOU STOP MISTAKING SHARED LONELINESS FOR LOVE

It takes sitting on her poncho in a park where mosquitos hunger
for skin before you believe

she is real
        believe she sees the fingerprints around what you are

and watches her own face change in the mirror
You know you are in love

with her then        when she says she wants to travel with you
        and you brave kissing her breasts where they peek

over tank top        exposed and *so close*        And suddenly
you are traveling in satellite orbit around her and her around you

as you go where night meets sea
        where your footsteps light up bioluminescence you aren't afraid of

because this light came out of you and could not possibly
mean you harm        And     you know this is faulty logic

        but like magic        you believe it anyway
After years        you are no longer moth to her intuitive flame

but fire yourself ready to fuel transformation
and celebrate these openings and closings and openings again

in this evolution of sex and love
There are miles and miles of foreplay

that need no destination;
there are love stories in the hollows of shoulders

while she sits across you on a massage table;
there are whole-body shakes

when she asks to share some of her being
and says     *that was only a teaspoon*

You want to tell her you love her
    and translate the energy

that fills every room you are in with her     —embodying
    luminous and alive—     but realize

that love poems to her are love poems to love itself     every word
an open portal to exactly this existence

## LAY WITH UNIVERSES ON THE BACKS OF YOUR EYES

You move into the heart of the house
        but this is still too open        vulnerable
            so you lock a lock you never knew
was there or suddenly appeared
and move into the bathroom
for another closed door          curve

around wall into bathtub
and shower curtain        mosaic light
dancing all the way down
a teal        paint-dusted drain     Three doorways
close before you are in too-hot water
        lungs breathing moisture instead of air

like in every dream you have of ocean
This cavernous bathtub spaceship
holds your folded limbs
in its amniotic fluid of awakening
        but you close your eyelids or maybe separate
from them altogether      broken rainbow light

streaming into this newfound underwater silence
You wonder how to interact
on the plane you step into     with pathways
of multicolored raindrops that vibrate

instead of pooling       *How could you all be*
*this alone together?*           Emerge

one layer at a time and return
from seeing through or inside reality
      —    ears releasing borrowed water    —
            and realize this whole house tilts
toward this drain      The bathtub
of your saltwater healing removes

the last shreds of pastel uncertainty
that you were ever anything except a being
skilled at leaving no trace      —or rather
leaving nothing in your wake that is not beautiful
        mesmerizing         aspiring to some ever-higher art form
of metaphysical communication

# TIME TO TURN CHAMELEON

You change colors when the sun
goes down or the camera turns on

      —wires crossed and rethreaded along your spinal column—
until you translate conservation into opulence

in a magical costume change        You remember
when manual gear shifts baffled you

—missing some muscle memory
your fingertips believe should be there—

and marvel at how exactly your scales color-match
now with digital accuracy        Truth is      aesthetics

is the best weapon against imposter syndrome
      but you already know that    —you've been impersonating

yourself long enough to remember

# SELF-SOVEREIGN

When you feel distance
                you venture
through this asteroid belt
of thoughts and into the foreign unknown
        some cosmic promise of

*out there*

When portals of smoke billow toward you

—they themselves gaseous stars
of exploded galaxies—

your rocketship swerves but

*sails on*

into wave vibrations of space
Here         there is little pleasure greater
than not needing to exit
states of pleasure as you determine
course through your evolved    —and therefore alien—
nature

# WHAT APPEARS TO BE DEATH

In this time machine spaceship of a body
        how often have you wondered what it would be like
to be free of it        floating

in the fluidity of air        dark or unaware
of your own consciousness        rising in a state of
utter relief

It's not always morbid        this    passing fascination
with what appears to be death        an ache
for whatever came before

you were urged toward flesh    When you die
in your dreams        —countless times now—        you don't just
experience
pain

but also something beyond that        something
imagined        perhaps        and intangible
                some notion
that    yes    here        —*finally*—

you're arriving at the destination you never strayed from
           your inner compass proved accurate at last
There are five seconds

to stop a bomb from going off in a parking lot
           which is only enough time to make peace with death
and feel the excitement seep

into your soon-to-be-bleeding heart        And when
the whole world explodes        you explode with it like the center
of a supernova star

           rippling time and space until you        too      are reduced
or perhaps elevated into some concept of measurement
           an instrument for consciousness

           a variable dependent on each electron for understanding
So      no      you suppose you are no longer afraid of what lies outside
the windows of this body

           and though you are in no certain rush to get there
                      it continues calling all the same

## DON'T LEAVE UNTIL THE CANDLE GOES OUT

You arrive
at your easternmost destination
and light four candles at a writer's grave
where you carry words inside you

like keys to doors you haven't found yet
In this nowhere town's graveyard where
anyone could be buried      there's a refinery
next door     and it's a wonder

the air doesn't catch flame     The wind blows out
one     two     three tealights until only one near his name
stands vigil to leftover tributes
—toy cars     coins         CDs—

left to soak up days-old rain
Maybe it is relentless
to come and claim what creativity he was channel for
       but you have asked bigger asks

and received them
There is already selenite balanced on marble like a spotlight
signal to Sirius to break
this reality you made for yourself

When you leave        you wonder if it is better
to be the inspiration or the herald
and think      *why not be both?*

so you carry this eternal torch
          creator again            —breathing fire
until everything speaks in tongues
of flame

## MIDNIGHT CREATORS' CONFERENCE


You gather on the equinox
where a woman holds a bottle up to camera light
and creates rainbows in these retina displays

where you are only hologram
      —experiment endowed with consciousness projected into morning
           filtered through lenses and layers over crystal

to form imagined solid
And now    too    the elusive dawn that is aurora in every language
—delicate to earth but strong to cosmos    You are all

those in this projection    mobiles of kaleidoscope transmissions
that ache to touch ground in your wandering for new angles
of the star storm that created you

      And    in the stillness of digital breath    you all begin
        to weave bells into blankets with well-worn fingers

# BE THE WORLD YOU WANT TO SEE CHANGE


You live for a tomorrow wider than wounds
you have worn          and this is what it means

to pre-tend utopia          Pre-tend the space where art springs
from your fingertips as you squirt paint

directly on your canvas          Pre-tend the world
where it is okay to be this happy

because no one suffering          where no one bears the pain
of a world wound          or if there is pain to be felt          let it be

honored          forgiven          moved through
all these widened channels of wishes          Pre-tend the romance

where you fall in love with your fingers          where
some inward sensation reminds you that every doorway

is a threshold          Pre-tend the awareness
where it is possible to hold space
          for every idea in its gestating rotations
Pre-tend pretending to pre-tend

such that you have done this before
and can offer yourself the advice of how to wander

in light          pre-tending the universe you create
when you open your hands in welcome

# ACKNOWLEDGMENTS

"Your Ancestors Are" (previously "Seven Swallowed Spiders") first appeared in *Sonic Boom*, issue 11

"Integrate" first appeared in *High Priestesses of Poetry: An Anthology*, Volume II

"Birth This Body" and "Particle Collison" first appeared in *Cauldron*

"Midnight Creators' Conference" (previously "In the Company of Priestess Women, I Remember I Am One") first appeared in *High Priestesses of Poetry: An Anthology*, Volume 1

The title, "Lay with Universes on the Backs of Your Eyes," is a line from a poem by Ash Good

The first lines in "Be the World You Want to See Change" are from the poem "Light" by Bernadette Miller

I also want to extend a big thank you to everyone who helped inspire and workshop these pieces, including Portland Women Writers, High Priestesses of Poetry, and Eastside Poetry Workshop.

**K. M. LIGHTHOUSE** is a queer poet and priestess creating portals for intuitive knowledge through writing spaces and workshops for self-healing. The poet has two other poetry chapbooks and a collage novel available: *You Are an Ambiguous Pronoun*, *The Observer Effect*, and *Time Counts Backward from Infinity*. Her other works appear in *The Florida Review* and *Toasted Cheese*.

www.ingramcontent.com/pod-product-compliance
Lightning Source LLC
Chambersburg PA
CBHW042130100526
44587CB00026B/4244